An Experiential View of Conflict in the Local Church

Focusing on Smaller and Medium-Sized Protestant Churches

by
Cleon E. Spencer

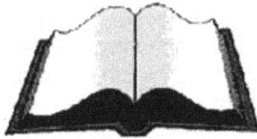

CCB Publishing
British Columbia, Canada

An Experiential View of Conflict in the Local Church:
Focusing on Smaller and Medium-Sized Protestant
Churches

Copyright ©2010 by Cleon E. Spencer
ISBN-13   978-1-926585-44-4
First Edition, Revised

Library and Archives Canada Cataloguing in Publication

Spencer, Cleon E.
An experiential view of conflict in the local church: focusing on
smaller and medium-sized Protestant churches /
written by Cleon E. Spencer.
ISBN 978-1-926585-44-4
1. Conflict management--Religious aspects--Protestant churches.
2. Interpersonal relations--Religious aspects--Protestant churches.
3. Church controversies. I. Title.
BV4597.53.C58S68 2009   254   C2009-904859-0

Publisher: CCB Publishing
               British Columbia, Canada
               www.ccbpublishing.com

To all the people who have been hurt in troubled congregations; and more especially to ministers whose career and person have been damaged, sometimes severely, this book is humbly and hopefully offered with heartfelt dedication.

Notes of Introduction
from the Author

The first notion I had of writing this book was to have it as a paper for a doctoral degree from a theological seminary at which I was studying. I was hoping to get some help from them on the mechanics of writing it. It was intended to be a writing mainly from my experiences. However, circumstances at the time side-tracked me into a more academic paper based on the writings of others.

Also, with the expressed opinion of a mentor that there is nothing new to write about on this subject, I put the idea of originality aside.

Now, twenty years or so later, more experienced, and getting into old age, I find myself taking up the topic again, and focusing on smaller to medium size congregations. Larger ones seem to have a wider choice of people to fill their various offices, and may therefore be less bothered by this problem, and less likely to be or remain smaller.

The writings in this book are not meant for

criticism but for constructive remedy. Also they are brief and to the point.

If a reader is looking for more elaborate writings on these and similar matters concerning difficult people, you may find help in two books previously written by this author. These books are available through most book stores. The titles are:

"THEY" CRIPPLE SOCIETY Volume One
- by Cleon E. Spencer

and

"THEY" CRIPPLE SOCIETY Volume Two
- by Cleon E. Spencer

Wishing you informative and meaningful reading with God's Blessing.

Cleon E. Spencer

Several Books have been written and published on the topic of local church conflict. The problem is often presented with resignation as an inevitable part of the process, with many ways offered to soften the blows that are sure to come, at least occasionally, sometimes frequently.

The GUIDELINES series of books by the United Methodist Church through its General Board of Discipleship offers much helpful, though incomplete discourse on the subject of a way of church administration that will help minimize conflict in a congregation.

Guidelines quotes the BOOK OF DISCIPLINE, 2000, as follows:

"The Pastor(s) shall oversee the total ministry of the local church in its nurturing ministries and in fulfilling its mission of witness and service in the world by: (1) giving pastoral support, guidance, and training to the lay leadership in the church, equipping them to fulfill the ministry to which they are sent as servants under the Lordship of Christ; (2) providing ministry within the congregation and to the world; (3) ensuring faithful transformation of the Christian faith; and (4) administering the temporal affairs of the congregation.
{The Book of Discipline of the United Methodist Church – year 2000 Page 217 Item 331}

One can see in this outline a flawless description of the role of the pastor to a congregation. The pastor, who is generally the person with the most training for ministry, has oversight of the congregation and all its activity. By this oversight he/she is not meant to do all the activity himself; nor is he meant to make all the decisions concerning this activity. Rather, he is meant to oversee and ensure that these decisions and the total ministry of the congregation by both ordained and lay ministry, is performed in compliance with the general beliefs and practices of the United Methodist Church at large.

This oversight of the congregation by the pastor makes way for the ministry of the Laity – another wonderful provision of GUIDELINES for the congregation through its local Church Council. The Church Council of a congregation is composed mainly of Lay people who are in positions of leadership in the various committees that together with the pastor, make up the Council. By way of seminars, workshops, and much printed material, training for these Lay Leaders is provided, mainly by the church at large.

The GUIDELINES booklet on CHURCH COUNCIL offers the basic training for Lay Leaders of the congregation. Its goal, among other things, wishes to train them as effective leaders. This it does effectively, to a point.

The result is we now have a congregation with a pastor trained as leader, and the chair of each committee trained as leader. Very little is said of how these leaders are to act and react together except to say that the Lay Leadership should keep in touch with the Pastor. This is vague and offers very little by way of allowing for the Pastor's oversight without treading on someone else's turf, so to speak. Some mention is made of the jealousy of some ministers to guard their turf.

Overall, the leadership plans are good as far as they go. A mature congregation could make a real going concern using the guidelines offered.

But – not all congregations are mature. What is it that makes a mature congregation? Mature, well informed people in charge of it, of course! It follows then that an immature congregation is inundated with some people including perhaps a minister occasionally who are ill-informed and/or immature in various ways.

These ill-informed and/or immature people and how they cause conflict in the local church will be the focus of this writing. It will also show how some of the conflicts are avoided or overcome, and some never are.

A subtitle of this book indicates it is mainly concerned with small to medium size churches. Large congregations generally have such a large assortment of mature leadership that the difficult people are outnumbered. Thus it has become a mature congregation. That doesn't mean to say that all smaller or medium size congregations are immature. Far from it. There are many other factors that come into play here. However, most of the congregations that do have an excess of conflict are smaller and or medium in size, and cannot be regarded as mature congregations. And there are exceptions to every rule.

To begin with, let us examine some case studies of how some churches handle delicate situations without harmful conflict and some do not.

* * * * *

A young minister with limited experience settled in as pastor of a congregation which some of its members regarded as a dying pastorate. The pastor was well received right at the start. Socially, the people of this medium size church were well cultured, mannerly people with whom the minister was well suited. Spiritually he was able to spark a renewed interest throughout the congregation and its history of more than a hundred years and then some. Obviously the people, among other good virtues, loved their church building, but not much work had been done on it in recent years. The pastor saw an opportunity in this.

At one of its earlier Board meetings, when there was an unplanned period of open, informal discussion, the pastor remarked, "You people have a historic church building here, and basically it is in good condition, and has the necessary facilities. Have you ever considered painting it up a little to make the sanctuary more cheerful and in keeping with our up-beat worship?"

There was dead-silence from the chairman. He appeared to be at a loss for words. The reaction of the others present was mixed but mostly positive. There were such remarks as, "We've never given it much thought." "It's a very high ceiling, high indeed. Can we do it with our limited finances?" A man with building experience responded, "Indeed we can do it. I myself would love to get at it, and a few other people with me who wouldn't be nervous about the height."

The interest grew throughout the community. Before long the interior of the sanctuary was renewed. Plans were forming to refurbish the exterior. The brick was in top condition, but the trim was in need of paint. The doors looked worn. The building already had outstanding stained glass windows that although generations old were well preserved. In the course of a few months an historic church was restored. Due to the ingenuity of the people, the financial cost was minimal. In addition, the congregation was infused with a renewed spirit.

During the process of the restoration, the Board chairman approached the Pastor one day. He told how glad he was to see the church of so many of their predecessors at last being rejuvenated. In a near to tears frame of mind he told the pastor how much it meant to him to see the old historic church of his forefathers being restored.

Then in words of remorse, he added, "As chairman of the board I should have had that all done some time ago, but I never gave it a thought that we could do it. "The pastor apologetically replied, "But I never meant to usurp you or interfere with your position on the Board." "Don't apologize," the chairman requested, "I support you all the way."

This man, instead of feeling hurt, or miffed or deflated, or with damaged pride, was very pleased and happy about it. The project didn't have to be to his credit. The church he loved was being renewed. Both the minister and the chairman and the whole board gave God the credit for moving them. No other credit was needed. He and that pastor remained life-long friends. Meanwhile, the chairman gave extra support through his giving of extra gifts of materials, at personal expense, to put the finishing touches here and there on the work of restoration.

What could have happened to the project, and to the congregation, if the chairman had not been the mature man that he was, can only be speculated upon. He could have guarded his position in the church as his turf, defied the minister who had not the slightest notion of encroaching on the turf of another. He could have divided the congregation on the issue. Instead, he helped to promote the whole idea, thus bringing unity to the community. He was a mature person, seeking to promote his church instead of himself.

From that time on, the congregation capitalized on its historicity, and the image it gave them. But that didn't cause them to dwell too much upon 'old times' as some such churches do. Their congregational programs for people of all ages are up there with the best of the more modern progressive churches

* * * * *

A young business oriented man and his wife, set up business in a town where they were known and largely respected. Things were going well for them. Being inclined towards their Christian faith they began attending church services and some other events as they gradually became more involved. In time the minister cooled towards them. This, in contrast to the fact that most other people solidly accepted them.

The minister's sermons gradually became more and more focused, as some ministers do, on the Christian Faith being for the poor. There were frequent reminders that Jesus was born in a stable, etc., etc.

This writer will elaborate on that piece of theology in a moment or two but for now only point out that this minister, like far too many of his colleagues was negative, very negative, on business and business people. It was obvious he knew very little about business, but he was against it anyway. Another example: there was a blast on one occasion, by an outstanding church official about a large corporation having a profit for the year, in the millions of dollars. It sounded as through it was an awfully greedy corporation. However research showed that the net profit for that very large corporation was only a small percentage and considered by most to be a reasonably safe profit margin – just enough to keep the corporation sound and secure in its operations. All the minister could see was the word millions. His sheer hatred for business, large and small, affected his relationship to the young business man toward whom he became negative. He obviously was down on people whom he thought, thought mind you, had money galore to shell out to the church, but were too stingy to give it. Of course there are some people stingy like that, but all too often, all business people are lumped into that category.

There is the saying that you can't logically be against something you don't know anything much about. And that is the way it is with far too many churches and their clergy. It would do well for some denominations to teach in their seminaries, in addition to theology, a mind broadening course in business principles and concepts; taught not by already biased theology professors, but by unbiased Christian business graduates who can present both sides of a situation.

The case just described and observed by this

writer happened half a century or so ago but has been widely repeated over the decades so much so that many larger and smaller business overlords have been alienated from various churches and the Christian ethics influence it could have had over business large or small. Some Christian lay-organizations have rescued a segment of these church castaways, and their fellowships are flourishing. Many churches with bias against business have failed society in this regard, and to this writer's mind, are in need of re-education on the subject.

* * * * *

A practical minded, and energetic pastor became the minister of a well worn congregation that had long ago become resigned to being a poor, small congregation with large buildings to keep up, as well as the expense of a minister's salary, and a few other items the treasurer dared to spend on.

The church funds were in the care of a treasurer of many years. He was well aware that the pastor's salary was of prime importance. So there was never a problem in that regard. But on other items he held the purse strings very tight, the same as if it were his own.

No doubt there is something to be admired

about a person so dedicated to the church as to care for the church finances, paying for its bare necessities, keeping it our of debt, facilitating its worship and other traditional activities of minimum expense.

Before the pastor had full knowledge of the financial circumstances, he had, from information given him by concerned parishioners, learned that the parsonage needed some work done on it before the cold winter. He checked it our and made a brief list of items needing improvement. He checked out the prices also. Being a handyman sort of person, he decided he would present the treasurer with an estimate for the building products only, and do the work himself. He would have time for that on this not real busy pastorate.

The treasurer received the estimate of less than one hundred dollars, a modest amount even at the time, with negativism and suspicion. He lectured the pastor on how a previous minister tried to pressure him on buying a new parsonage. He emphasized that they would never get out of debt again if they did and hoped that request doesn't arise again.

The pastor agreed that this pastorate could not afford such a venture as to buy a new house. He made no further requests to the negative treasurer for money of any amount. He decided to buy the needed material with his own money. He did so and in a matter of weeks had the work completed. The winter was cold but the parsonage was comfortable, To make matters better one of the groups of the congregation reimbursed the pastor for the money he had spent, and added more materials to that, all paid for by the church group. Twenty five years later that same house was still in use as the comfortable parsonage of that pastorate. But the damage was done.

From then on the treasurer was cold and unaccepting of the pastor. The treasurer wasn't in full control any more. Such is the behavior of people who feel they have to be in control. Two nearby influential people with whom the treasurer had close contact also grew cold toward this pastor. They somehow perceived that the pastor was being harsh toward the treasurer. Actually he made every effort to please the treasurer. The case really was, the new pastor was just too much for the treasurer. And nothing seemed to help. The parsonage had been made warm and comfortable. But the atmosphere of the pastorate had been chilled. In a few peoples eyes including the two influential people, there should be request for a new pastor. The majority of the congregation was well pleased with the pastor they had. However, the minority sided with those who held that the pastor was being harsh on the treasurer – a mistake often made in church quarrels, and accepted by the hierarchy as being the cause of the problem.

If these nearby people of influence had not been biased concerning their attitude towards the new pastor who could turn his hand to just about anything, steps could be invoked to restore trust and peace to the pastorate, which in turn would allow it to prosper within its potential. However, it didn't happen that way. That pastorate barely survived and continued for many years with its nip-and-tuck budget. Even troubled churches with enough good people in them have a way of survival that many other organizations would love to have. Such was the case here.

However, the parsonage was now a comfortable home for future pastors for years to come. That aspect of the story received no attention at all. Yet, there were those who erroneously held only that the pastor who made it so for them had been harsh on the treasurer. As the vernacular saying would put it, "it was his problem." That is to say, it was the treasurer's problem, not the minister's. Had there been the right kind of help available to help the treasurer adjust to a new, progressive ministry, harmony could have been established.

* * * * *

There was a minister experienced in most phases of church work, a sound, mind-captivating preacher, thrifty in his attitude toward church finances, of pleasant, well behaved character, and well liked by the majority of people he came in contact with.

He became pastor of a medium size congregation which was well organized with leaders of its many programs, some of whom were well qualified because of their employment in executive positions of varied levels. There also were people of other various levels of the career world. Their skills could be useful in any church. Could be that is!

Early in his ministry there the pastor experienced good response from the people generally. There was a marked increase in attendance at worship. The pastor reached out to the few people who had not been attending regularly, and brought them back. He planned that in time he would reach out to the new residential areas on the outskirts of the community. In the meantime he focused on the various outreach activities of the church, and working along with the lay leaders in charge of them. Most of them, men and women, were good to work with. Most of them, that is!

There was a small nucleus of lay leaders, just a few, who were at first difficult to read. At meetings they had little to say except a yes or no, or criticism or addition to what someone else, especially the pastor, had proposed. In time it became more noticeable to the pastor.

It became obvious that these few people acted as though they were the leaders of the congregation as a whole, and everything done must have their approval These were well educated people, doing well in the secular world, in positions of leadership. They wanted to utilize their leadership role in the church in a condescending way. They were proud of their humility towards the church. Their attitude seemed to be that their pride must not be shaken. The pastor was careful at the time not to do so.

As the minister focused on the more compatible leaders and the general membership of the congregation, the activity of the pastorate flourished, and most people were happy about it. Their spiritual lives were in good form. They showed affection toward their pastor, and he handled it well. The members of the other nucleus grew more cold and overbearing generally. But the minister would not let their overbearing attitude get the better of him. He refused to succumb to such immature behavior. In time he would have to stand up to them. He may not accomplish much in such an atmosphere, but he wouldn't be brought low either. As often happens the larger portion of the congregation didn't know what was going on. The wayward lay leaders group, small though it was, were well entrenched. They were now giving the minister the cold shoulder and making things uncomfortable for him in ways that need not now be described. To make a long story short, the pastor was eventually squeezed out.

That pastorate continued with its status quo until it became a congregation focused on survival. Those who caused it to be so, later received high accolades of approval for still standing by their church even when it was going down.

*****

A small town was fast becoming a city suburb. Its small town church needed to keep up or be lost in the shuffle. The new minister was all ears as he listened to the more progressive members stating that a new building was needed to enhance the already existing premises. He surveyed the circumstances, and consulted with a supervisor of the church at large, who approved.

However, there was opposition. It came from the 'old school' who wanted the church to remain small, easy to manage, and under their control. On the other hand there were numerous people of good caliber who were anxious to see it go ahead. These included people who knew a lot more about building than did the pastor. He gladly utilized all their skills, bringing them together in unity of spirit.

The old congregation was overruled and the project went ahead. There was no self-centered pride in the way now. No one trying to take credit or be heard over the others. No one insisting on his or her own way. The objective was to make, not themselves, but their church, first and foremost a credit to the community that was evolving.

Of course, the whole project was a resounding experience for those who got involved. They grew in spirit and experience, and became more useful people in the community at large.

When a project like that is taken on in the church it is almost sure to produce people of leadership qualities in the secular community as well. Many years later that local church is still flourishing; not just surviving. It is a vibrant influence and example, in its own community, but also in the church at large.

* * * * *

A fledgling congregation met and elected an administrative board with a chairperson and other necessary officers such as treasurer, and so on. A new minister then arrived on the scene. He was much experienced in small church administration, and so set about to streamline the functioning of the church. There was no outright verbal opposition to this, but there was a coldness, and a sense of dissatisfaction about the atmosphere.

In time the minister quoted that part of the Book of Discipline which read, "The pastor shall oversee the total ministry of the church in its nurturing ministries---giving pastoral support, guidance, and training to the lay leadership in the church. (The Book of Discipline of the United Methodist Church. Year 2000 Page 217, item 331). From there on things gradually brightened up, and in time, as they got to know and trust each other, it became clear that previously they had pictured the set up in an erroneous manner. They had seen the chairperson of the board as the ministers boss, with the minister as their employee. The Treasurer also figured large in this set up since he was the one who paid the minister.

However, it wasn't a power trip as sometimes occurs in a congregation. It was a case of being ill informed, which had the person with the most training, the pastor, taking his orders from those with little or no training.

No harm was meant by anyone involved. In a short time an administration was running smoothly. The pastor changed or added nothing without placing it before the Board for discussion and approval or rejection. Likewise, the Board chair and other members changed or added nothing without it being brought before a meeting of the board, at which the pastor was present. This arrangement was utilized without distress for the several years of that ministry. The pastor and the chairman became life long friends. The other members of the Board were like members of a very close family. There was not an incident of discord over a period of the several years of that ministry.

Having examined how some churches handle difficult situations successfully, and some are less fortunate with it, let us now examine many various types of difficult characters that are likely to be involved, one way or another, in an assortment of difficult situations.

* * * * *

A minister has taken up ministerial duties on his/her first pastorate. He is eager to experience the role of leader of a congregation and to convince himself that he can do the full work of ministry. I would say he has a right to feel that way at that point in his career. It belongs to human nature. Nowadays, a much more thorough, hands on training is given to beginners, regardless of age. And that is a great help.

However, to lead a congregation doesn't mean for one person, namely this minister, to direct all the activities, and expect all others to follow. It has to be a shared direction with the officers that have been designated by the congregation itself. In order for this sharing to work well over a long period of time, there has to be tact and diplomacy, and giving and taking on both sides, but especially on the part of the pastor. And there has to be a democratic process, strictly adhered to, of speaking and voting. If the pastor becomes too overbearing, and especially if he is overbearing on some questionable plans or proposals, his leadership may come into question.

On the other hand, there are congregations, and even more so church administrative boards that have a long established resentment toward the minister having much input at all into the administration of the local church. They see him/her as the preacher and only the preacher. They refer to him as the preacher, but leave no room for him to be otherwise. In some congregations the minister is affectionately referred to as the preacher, but at the same time, his total oversight of the congregational activities is fully recognized and appreciated. On the other hand there are congregations where the minister is regarded as the preacher only. He is expected to be under the oversight of the local church board and do their bidding in all else. This is unfair to the minister, since he has training in all aspects of church development. There should be a balance, as delicate as it may be at times, between the ordained, more highly trained leader and the lay leadership.

When that balance isn't present then serious conflict may arise between the minister and his supporters, and the remainder of the church administrators; either that or one side lets the other side always have its way. In this case the administration as a democratic body becomes ineffective, with the congregation itself splitting apart, with a substantial number of members dropping away, over time. Conflict will again have taken its toll.

* * * * *

Any minister who is fortunate enough to have a well experienced, well charactered corporate executive as the chairperson of his local church Board, is fortunate indeed. However, to be the head of a secular corporation is one thing, an honorable thing indeed but to be the head of a church Board is another altogether, and requires some adjustment. Putting a product or a service of good value on the market can be a Christian calling indeed – a way to make life better for people. Putting Christianity on the market is also a way to make people better for life.

A minister takes up his duties anew on a pastorate that has such a corporate executive who has been chairperson of the Board for considerable time. This congregation has maintained its status quo as a carefully managed organization.

Although this pastorate is maintaining itself well it is no longer relevant to the times in which it now finds itself. The area has mushroomed with new housing and an increasing population. The new minister has the training and experience in church growth to enlarge the ministry of this congregation, rather than simply just minister to its past and present.

The minister treads lightly for a while, until he has the acceptance and liking of the congregation as a whole. Then he begins to make suggestions for growth. Although these suggestions are well thought of by people who liked the minister, and would hopefully be accepted by the Board, such was not the case. As carefully and gradually as the minister tried to prepare for expansion, the corporate executive Chair of the Board became miffed at having what he now obviously regarded as his turf being invaded. It obviously was upsetting him. In addition some other members of the Board sympathized with the chairman being upset by this minister whom they saw as being too ambitious. So there came to be divided allegiance among the Board members, which before long affected the congregation. Further conversations pertaining to the matter revealed that it was too much for many of them to visualize.

Almost no one, including the minister wanted to take sides in a potential church split. That church didn't progress with the community growth around it. Undisciplined pride was protected throughout the Board. A well run status quo continued. And another congregation of the church missed a wonderful opportunity.

* * * * *

Then there is the pastor who is very proud of his/her position as leader and lecturer (preacher) to a significant size body of people. He can be, at times, as proud as a peacock, and is not the least humbled by his call from God. In all aspects of his work, he has to feel he is top dog. His usual behavior in the pulpit and at meetings is "laying it on the line" as the vernacular would put it.

This minister guards his wrongly perceived position with envy. Especially when there is input from some of the smart members of the Board, rivalry sets in. Then the participants on the Board have to either give in to him, perhaps even cower before him, or, quarrel with him. Either way, ill feeling sets in. And so it goes again; if the Board members have to give in to him to keep the peace, an unhealthy atmosphere of discontent is created to the detriment of the church. If the Board members stand up to him and insist on being heard, the erring minister's pride is punctured, and quarreling is sure to set in. He may even promote the notion that he is being mistreated. Hurt pride and its ensuing envy and rivalry can take some strange twists; very strange indeed, even twists that are paranoid.

* * * * *

There was a pastorate with a smart but overbearing Chairperson who had largely ruled over the congregation for some time. She hadn't gotten along well with the previous minister, and now there was a new minister for her congregation.

This new minister, as his experienced custom was, at first merely sat in on meetings and mostly listened, except for minor information and clarification along the way. His ministry was extremely well received by the congregation and by the townsfolk as they came to know him, and he them. In due time, however, he began to notice that his popularity may be bothering the Chairperson.

No pastor can sit in on meetings indefinitely without participation in ideas and debates on the topics of discussion. As this pastor began to participate more and more, the chairperson became more and more jumpy with him, as though his comments and ideas were too much for her to handle. In time she began to counteract his opinions in a nervous sort of way.

To bring the story fast forward some, it came to be that she and some of her allies would try to block anything the pastor tried to say. If he put forward an idea, and sometimes there were tried and tested good ones, it would be treated as insignificant. Belittling was setting in.

This minister wasn't one to be walked over lightly. Over time he reacted by paying little attention to the bogus rubber stamp meetings, and went about a ministry of his own, apart from the Board as much as possible; for example by having his own Bible study Group. Altogether, this salvaged the ministry of the pastor, but it also punctured the long standing pride of the chair-person and her allies. The pastor stood his ground and refused to be subdued by them. Their pride was upset all the more. As happens, envy followed by rivalry soon has set in and there was conflict between the pastor and the part of the Board, a significant part, that sided with the chairperson. The remainder of the Board members were more or less subdued or didn't know what to do about it. Much of the congregation wasn't aware of what was happening. The pastor was able for the chairperson, and most of the time could check her and keep her in her place.

That caused serious problems. The chairperson and her allies resorted to a defense that trouble makers often use. They turn the whole matter around and blame the whole problem on the person who is on the defensive and winning over them. They were now pointing the finger and saying in effect, "just look what the pastor is doing to her."

The pastor was only defending himself and his career. They now interpreted that as the pastor treating the chairperson badly. Reports of it got to the church hierarchy. The pastor received phone calls from administrative officials whom he didn't know, asking what he was doing to those people. There were noticeably no offers of professional help to try to bring reconciliation; there was only blame on the pastor. The punctured pride of the chairperson and her allies, and the ensuing envy and rivalry that emanates from it, was now full fledged to the point of paranoia on their part. They thought the minister was doing them wrong. He was only defending himself.

This minister made attempts to clear his name in the church at large, but found there was absolutely no understanding of the problem. His efforts to get a fair hearing were shunned, as he was personally. His career would never be the same again. Wrongly understood conflict in the local church had taken its toll once more. Another career was severely damaged, and nobody knew the difference between the right and wrong of it. With some individual exceptions, this particular area of the church at large knew everything but people!

* * * * *

In some other congregations we have those lost souls who are always looking for another minister, the 'right' minister – whom they never do find, but for whom they keep on looking.

There was a medium size congregation with a lot going for it. They had had a live-wire minister who did wonderful things to activate and bring this church into the mainstream. His preaching and other worship activities were always meaningful and of interest to most members of the congregation – to most of them that is.

There was this little nucleus, just a few malcontents and any minor support they were able to muster. They nudged and nagged until they got rid of the effective minister. He moved to another more appreciative congregation. The congregation he had just left was now unable, for some time, to attract a high caliber minister. When they finally did, it was only a matter of time before the club of malcontents, a definite minority, began their game of discontent again.

What these people are looking for is not impossible to determine. When a new minister questioned them as to what they expected in a pastor, they told him this, that, and the other thing. The new pastor reminded them that they had all those things in a previous pastor whom they got rid of previously and that they must have made a mistake in getting rid of him. They replied that they had indeed made a mistake not realizing what they had at the time. The present pastor continued to press them further by reminding them that even though the congregation had now picked up, and was presently going well again, they were now doing the same thing over, in trying to get rid of the present minister. When asked what reasons they could give for this they gave rather irrational answers.

The reasons they gave were mainly that they would like a preacher who preaches form the Bible, like we see on television; Bible in hand, and turning the pages as you go. And they hope at the same time to see more animation and movement around the church. It would be exciting and take away their boredom.

The pastor informed them that type of preaching is not common in our denomination. When questioned further their response amounted to the fact that they did not want to change to another denomination. It seems they wanted to change this present congregation to meet their personal needs for excitement in worship, rather than a basically meaningful type of service. One fact for sure is, they did not want to go elsewhere to church because they were also control freaks and wanted to continue to control what they had. People were not wise to them in that regard.

The majority by far of the congregation was content with their church on the track it was on, and with the ministries it had. Yet, these excitement seeking control freaks stirred and nudged and maneuvered over a long period of time, until the good pastor left them. Then they were able to start, all over again their game of discontent, and seeking for the right minister. Malcontents are never content for long, and only then if the can carry the minister in their pocket, under complete control; and his family with him if they can. Yes, and there are still a few "traditional" cronies who insist that the minister's wife should not be employed outside the home and church; not even after her family has grown up. She should be busy at all times in the church under their tutelage. Such a practice sometimes reduced the spouse to a church flunky. That practice disappeared at least fifty years ago or more. But there are a few even now who think it should still stand.

Sometimes such people as described above, seek to supervise the minister. They may have little or no experience or training in supervising employees, but here is their chance. Often the best they can do is give orders in a clumsy sort of way. To make matters worse, if there are those among them that do physical work for a living, often highly skilled, middle class work nowadays, and they erroneously have the idea that book and paper work, such as a minister does for a living is easy, or not really work at all. Therefore the minister should be available at all times for whatever tasks they may ask of him. If he lets them they can run him ragged in no time at all; if he doesn't go along with it he may be regarded as either lazy, or uncooperative.

There is, in some congregations, the critic and corrector who expects perfection of the minister. In their supervision of him they are ready to correct, even jump on him at the least little error. This action adds authenticity to the critic's supervision – so he/she thinks; giving a sense that there is a need for such supervision. If the pastor were to pay much attention to this he would need to allow himself to become a perfectionist, which by the way, is not a healthy way to live.

Leading a congregation as either a lay or ordained person of the church is, more or less, an executive position, with how much so depending on the size of the congregation. This writer's experience has taught that in most smaller congregations, more is accomplished through informal and largely unstructured discussion around a kitchen table, than at a strictly chaired formal meeting. In this informal manner, openness is largely unhindered, and topics of all sorts are brought to light. Many items are pretty well settled before the formal meeting comes. Then only an occasional formal meeting is required to adjust and make official the kitchen table decisions.

Nevertheless, in even a little larger, more active congregations more structure is a necessity, and that requites varying measures of humble executive abilities. For persons who do not have such experience, the church, regardless of size, can be a wonderful training ground. I have known people who have gained such level-headed experience in the church for a few years and then moved on to take leadership positions in the immediate community, and upward from there, for the good of the general life of the whole area.

However, when one uses such opportunity and

experience to vaunt oneself and one's position over others, in selfish ambition, as happens more often that is should, then the whole process is in vain.

What is needed to prevent this, is more emphasis on Judeo-Christian character within and throughout the church. In many areas, emphasis on character is in short supply. There are cases where congregations are swamped in enmity, hard feelings and rivalry. This is not just because of differences of opinion, but because of lack of Judeo-Christian character at work in dealing with people and issues. The characteristics of such character is a whole other topic. In the meantime in our experiences in the church congregation we can see areas where correction of character is in need, and also where good well founded character is a wonderful asset and blessing to the work of the church.

* * * * *

Concerning the rich and the poor and the church, the negative on business Christians have some favorite, though misunderstood claims to promote their mistaken theology and cause problems in the church. That Jesus was born in a stable is a frequent one. But Jesus was born in a stable, not because Joseph didn't have any money, or was too poor to pay for a room. Jesus was born in the stable, because the Inn was filled up. There were no vacancies. In this twenty first century similar happens to people in busy tourist areas during vacation season, and we sometimes have had to sleep in our car. It has happened to this writer on occasion.

Indications are that Joseph carried on his trade as a carpenter – a prominent trade of that time and now, and also sufficiently remunerative then and now to promote a good living.

The shepherds were at the stable on the night of Jesus' birth. Because of this the negatives claim that Jesus came to the poor people. The shepherds weren't necessarily poor. Being a shepherd was a skilled occupation of that time, as it is today. Shepherds had to know the animals for which they cared; how to sufficiently see they are adequately fed; when and when not to shear them of their wool; how and when to market the wool; when and when not to slay them for meat; what choice of grazing land is best for them at what season. It was the equivalent of a skilled trade of the twenty first century, and was likely also sufficiently remunerative for a good living. Present day people making a living from sheep can tell you of the skills required. I had occasion to observe it for myself.

Yes, the shepherds certainly were at the stable

on that first Christmas, They were representative of the middle class of their time. But so were the three Kings there. God sent his Son, Jesus, for all peoples – shepherds and kings and all in between. There was no bias on God's part. He is there for all who open their hearts to Him in sincerity and love. For those who miss out on the abundant life for one reason or another, often not their own fault, God commands us to care for the poor, seeking to lift them up to the more abundant life.

Abraham, called by God, is said to have been a person of wealth, having his own entourage of security attendants and associates, said by some to be the equivalent of a sizable army and support system for that time.

Job was certainly wealthy. He remained faithful to God when he lost all he had. God later restored his fortunes, and Job declared God as his living redeemer.

Numerous people of the Bible were people connected to wealthy or well-to-do families; wealthy in ways that constituted wealth at that time.

* * * * *

We are commanded by God to care for the poor. However, Jesus said, that the poor you have with you always, but look what this person did to me! We are bound to look after the poor and lift them up wherever possible. But we are not called to build our whole religious faith on our work for the poor. They are just one facet of our ministry, as important as that facet is.

At one time when I ministered in an area where it was common for clergy while on duty to wear a clerical collar, I had an interesting experience concerning the poor. I went alone into a restaurant for lunch. The booths were all filled. However there were stools vacant at the snack bar, so I sat there, a space or two from a friendly man. He spoke to me saying, "You're busy today looking after the poor are you?"

I replied, "No, it's the sick and the distressed today."

"But," he remarked, "most of your work is with the poor, is it not?"

Again, I replied, "Well, I have some work reaching out to the poor, but I guess I'm fortunate to have a congregation in which most are well-to-do people." Then I took control of the conversation: "You seem to think the only work of the church is with the poor."

"That's been my experience," he said, and continued, "I'm fairly well off financially, but when I ventured to align myself with a church, the only interest they had in me was my money to help the poor. Had I stayed with them I very soon would have become poor myself. So no more church for me."

"I think you were in a misguided church, a church that has been misguided by the new and wayward and overly liberal theology," I tried to reassure him.

A lengthy conversation didn't rescue him. His experience was an intense one that taught him he must give away his money to the poor, to the point of becoming poor himself. He was a smart man who had worked hard for his money. He was willing to share a reasonable portion of it, but not hand it out freely to people, many of whom do not even give life a good try.

The church is not only for helping the poor, as someone had tried to lead him to believe. The church is for everybody, including successful entrepreneurs, and also those who didn't make the grade for one reason or another.

* * * * *

Even the dead can be the cause of conflict in the local church! The established denominations of the church, have in their various resources, adequate guidance for funerals in their churches. These resources usually provide much room for variety and diversity to take care of special wishes and concerns of family and friends involved.

However, often as a funeral is planned we have people who have attended many, many funerals in a variety of denominations and congregations, and, different than them all, many funerals in independent churches in which the pastor has developed his/her own style and content.

And then there are those who are afraid the minister will use a funeral sermon of hell-fire and brimstone to scare people into being 'saved'. Also, there are people who want the pastor to utilize that same tactic to get relatives of the deceased saved. No thought that the minister might have some idea of his own on the matter.

Again, some want only tributes and reflections concerning the deceased, which is okay as far as it goes. But they give no thought that the pastor may want to say something concerning what God's Word says about life and death, for the purpose of comfort to the bereaved.

So people may on occasion request a funeral with this and that in it like they have over at such and such a church across town. Such people have no thought that such a request may be an affront to the denomination which has its own well developed and distinct type of funeral. The minister is often bombarded with requests for funerals that are so foreign they have little or no similarity to the usual for their denomination. Even when the pastor bends a long way to please them, some people, when they don't get their way in demanding their own type of funeral, stir up bad feelings that are carried over to disturb the peace of the local church.

Conclusion

Reflecting on this writer's observations and experiences: if a mature minister is fortunate enough, early in his/her career to find himself / herself in a mature congregation, it is much more certain that such a minister will be getting off to a good start for a mature ministry throughout their career.

If a not so mature minister gets even a pretty good church, when trouble arises, or the church diminishes, not if, but when, there is a high risk that the congregation will take the blame.

If a very mature minister gets a very immature congregation they will try, at least, to walk all over him/her, and he/she will take the blame. It will appear to be so to people who are not people wise, or not street smart. The minister may appear to some of them as not strong enough for the task.

In such cases, the minister, hopefully with the sanction of the superiors of the church at large, should walk away from such confrontation. Not that it is impossible to fix in a manner suggested herein, but it would take, not months, but sometimes years to do so. The severe stress and strain of it could waste away ones career. A different type of minister may fit in there quite well perhaps, with a different type of ministry. And the exiting minister could be fitted into a more compatible pastorate a convenient distance away.

A significant portion of the church at large presently is not street smart enough to decipher all the circumstances. So, many good people, ordained and lay, are short changed in life and in the church, and perhaps driven away.

These are generalities. However, there are exceptions to every rule. Some of these exceptions come through tactful and timely interventions by fair-minded persons of insight and influence.

Nonetheless, people are people. How can the circumstances be changed for better, so that good people don't come off with the worst of it, as happens all too often?

This writer would like to see that therapeutic support groups become commonplace throughout the denominations that are plagued by these problems. Such support groups would have to be monitored by mature Christian counselors, therapists, or coaches, who are well developed in faith based counseling and Judeo-Christian character, familiar with the general workings of a congregation, and are also worldly wise (street smart) to the pitfalls human nature can either fall into or be overwhelmed by. Therapists with theoretical ideas about such matters will not do.

As long as there are people there will be people problems. However, this writer believes that with open minds much improvement can be made in the areas of Judeo-Christian character and Christian behavior towards others in the church and in the world.

God's grace and a love for the church that rises above self can make it so.

The End

* 9 7 8 1 9 2 6 5 8 5 4 4 4 *